A FILM BY STEVEN SPIELBERG

SCHINDLER'S LIST
PIANO SOLO

COMPOSED BY

JOHN WILLIAMS

ISBN 978-0-7935-3277-3

HAL•LEONARD®
CORPORATION
7777 W. BLUEMOUND RD. P.O. BOX 13819 MILWAUKEE, WI 53213

Visit Hal Leonard Online at
www.halleonard.com

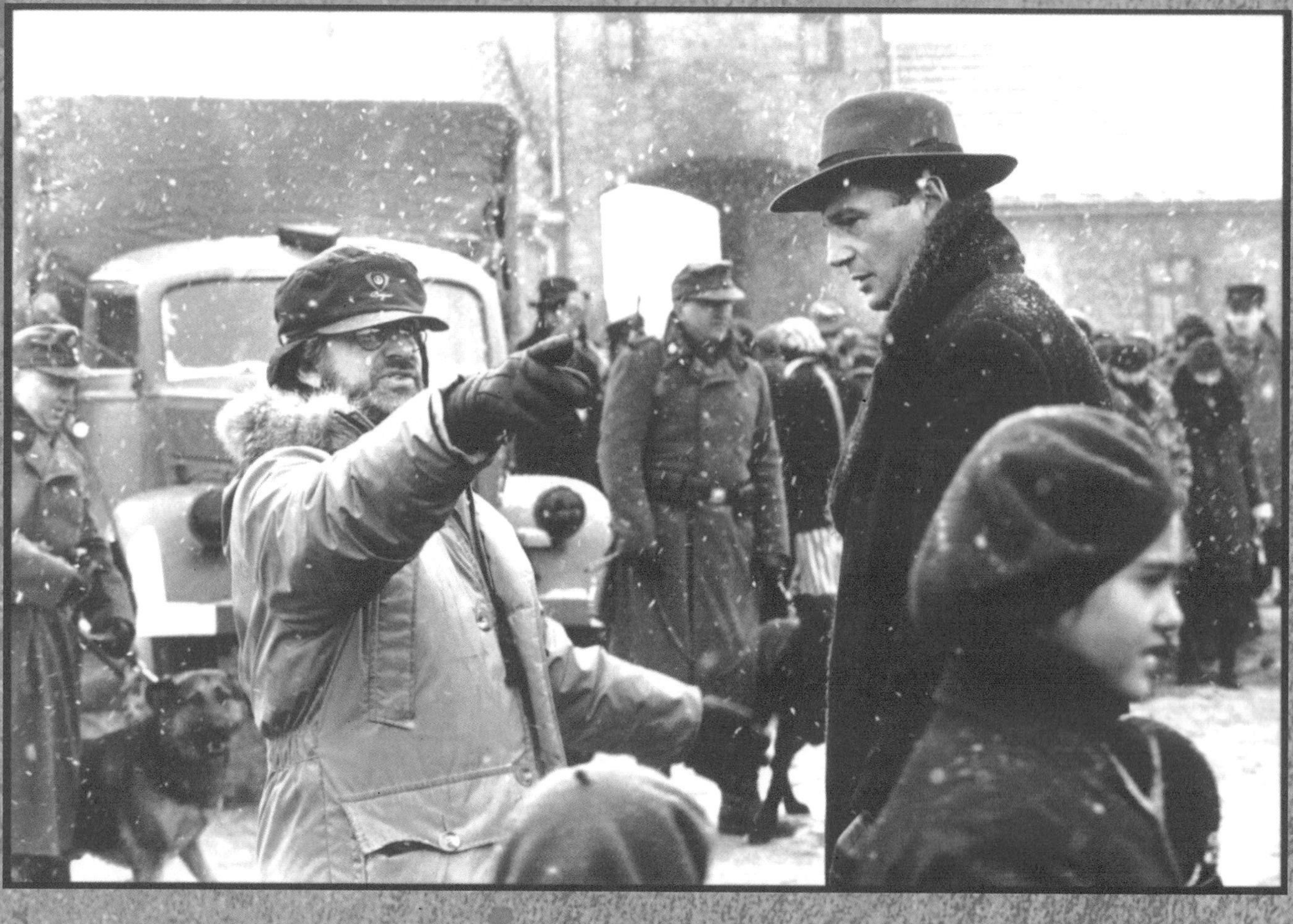

A FILM BY STEVEN SPIELBERG
SCHINDLER'S LIST

CONTENTS

JEWISH TOWN
(KRAKOW GHETTO - WINTER '41)

Composed by
JOHN WILLIAMS

Reflectively

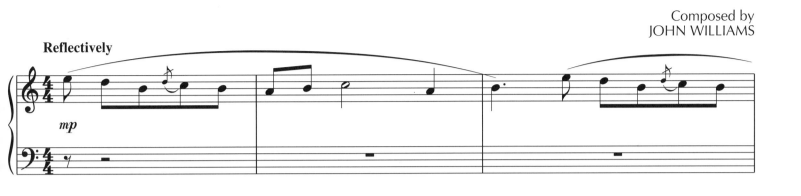

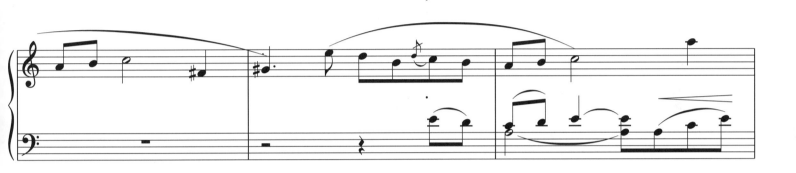

IMMOLATION
(WITH OUR LIVES, WE GIVE LIFE)

Composed by
JOHN WILLIAMS

Slowly, but with motion

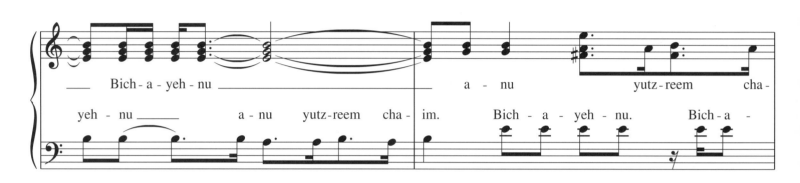

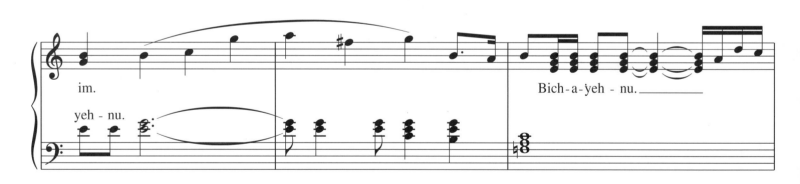

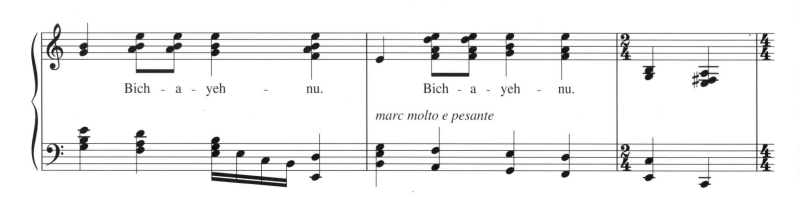

REMEMBRANCES

Composed by
JOHN WILLIAMS

cresc.

dim.

(bring out melody, expressively)

dim.

p

I COULD HAVE DONE MORE

Composed by
JOHN WILLIAMS

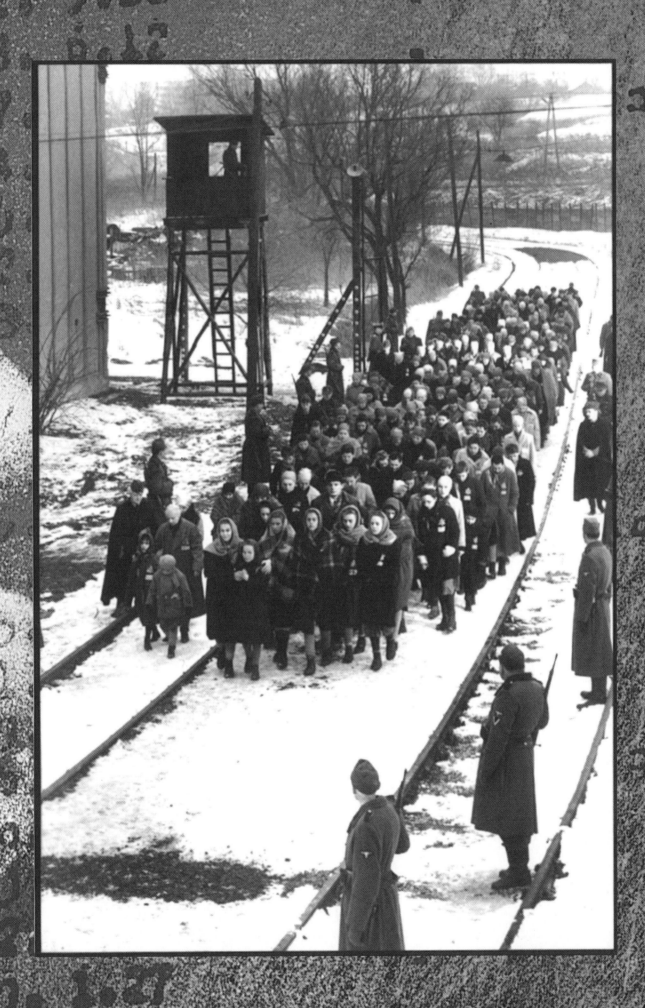

STOLEN MEMORIES

Composed by
JOHN WILLIAMS

MAKING THE LIST

Composed by
JOHN WILLIAMS

Slowly

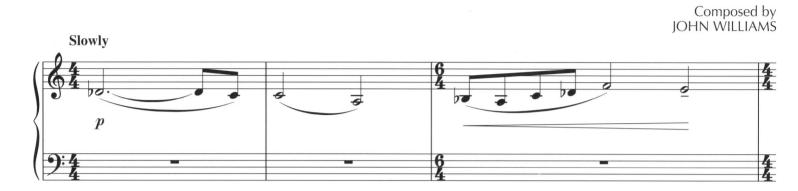

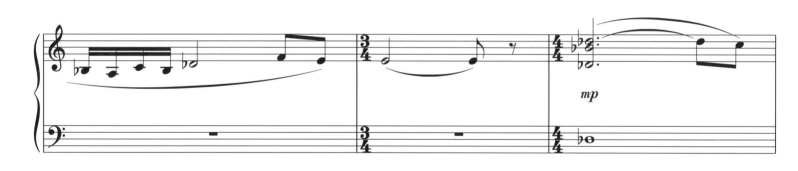

GIVE ME YOUR NAMES

Composed by
JOHN WILLIAMS

THEME FROM "SCHINDLER'S LIST"
(Reprise)

Composed by
JOHN WILLIAMS